DOT TO DOT
FARM LIFE
FOR ADULTS

This book includes 30 Unique Dot Pages.

Start from 1st Number dot and continue all the way till you reach end of numbers, all the designs are continous lines and there are no jumps or breaks!

If you have any suggestions or ideas, please drop an email to
info@coloringbooks101.com

Copyright © 2021 by Sonia Rai

TABLE OF CONTENTS

Boy Feeding Cow (509 dots) - Black

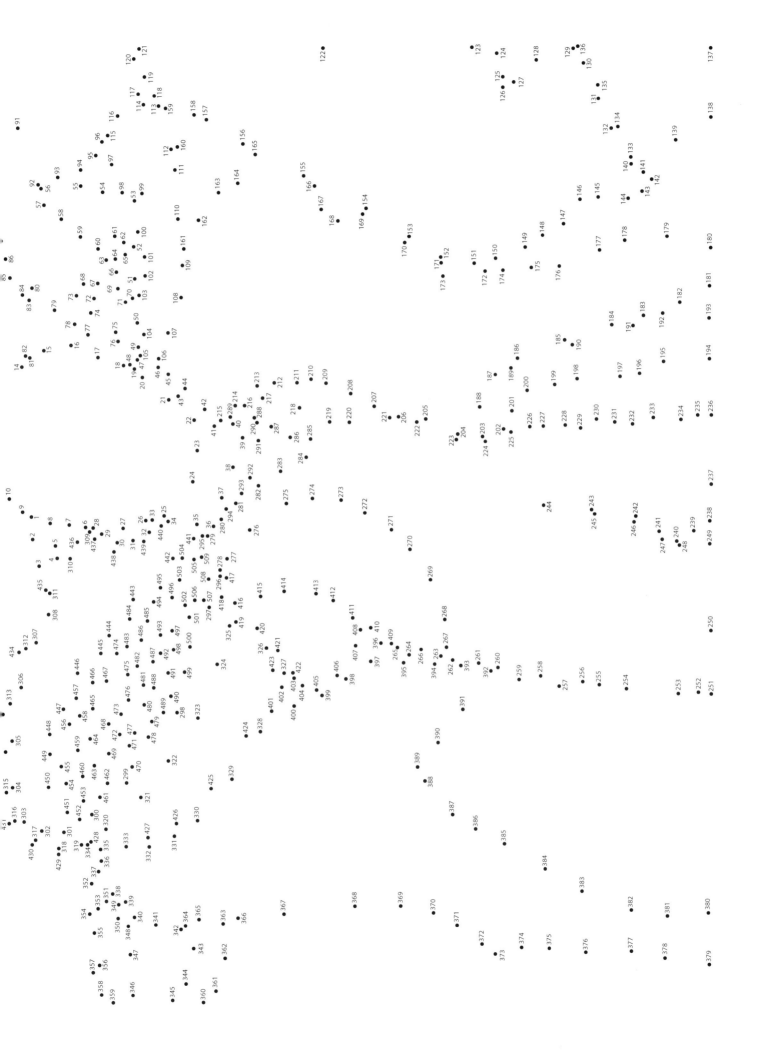

Couple Farming Seeds (650 dots) - Black

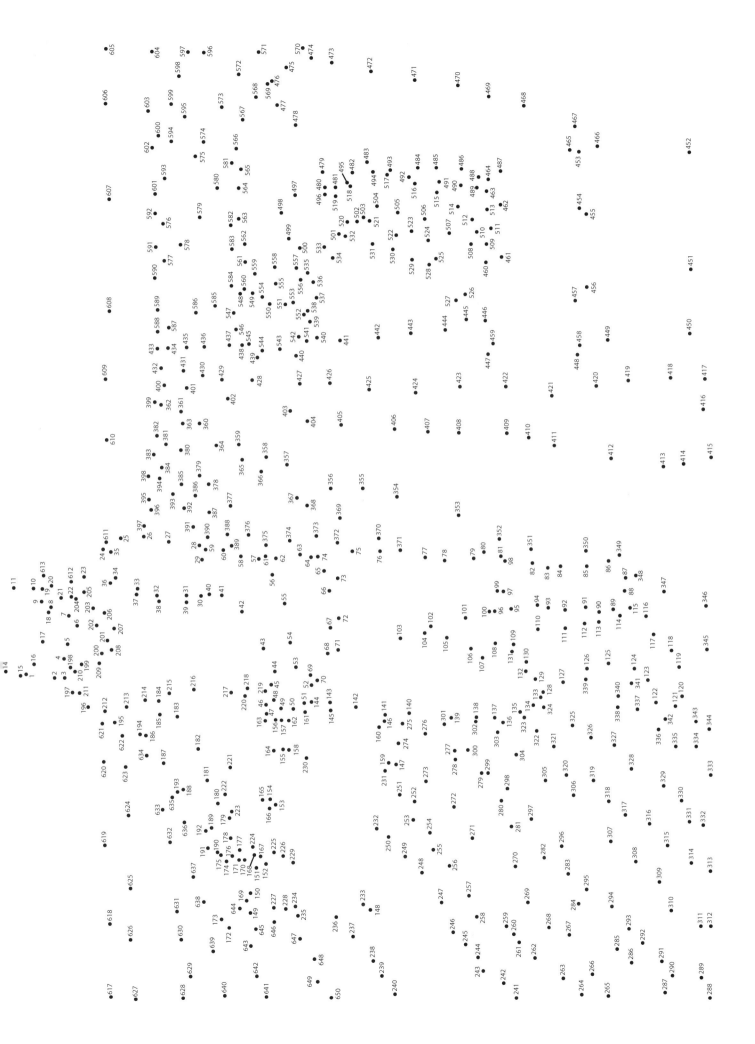

Cow (456 dots) - Black

Cow In Farm Shed (475 dots) - Black

Cows in Farm (505 dots) - Black

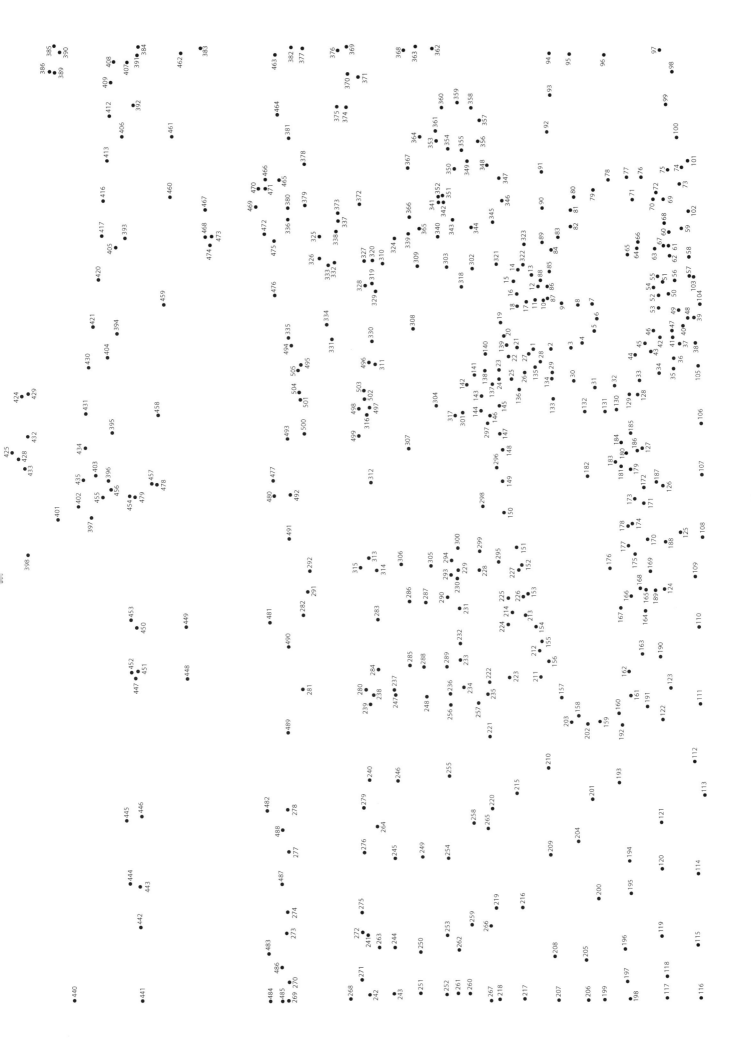

Dog in Farm (665 dots) - Black

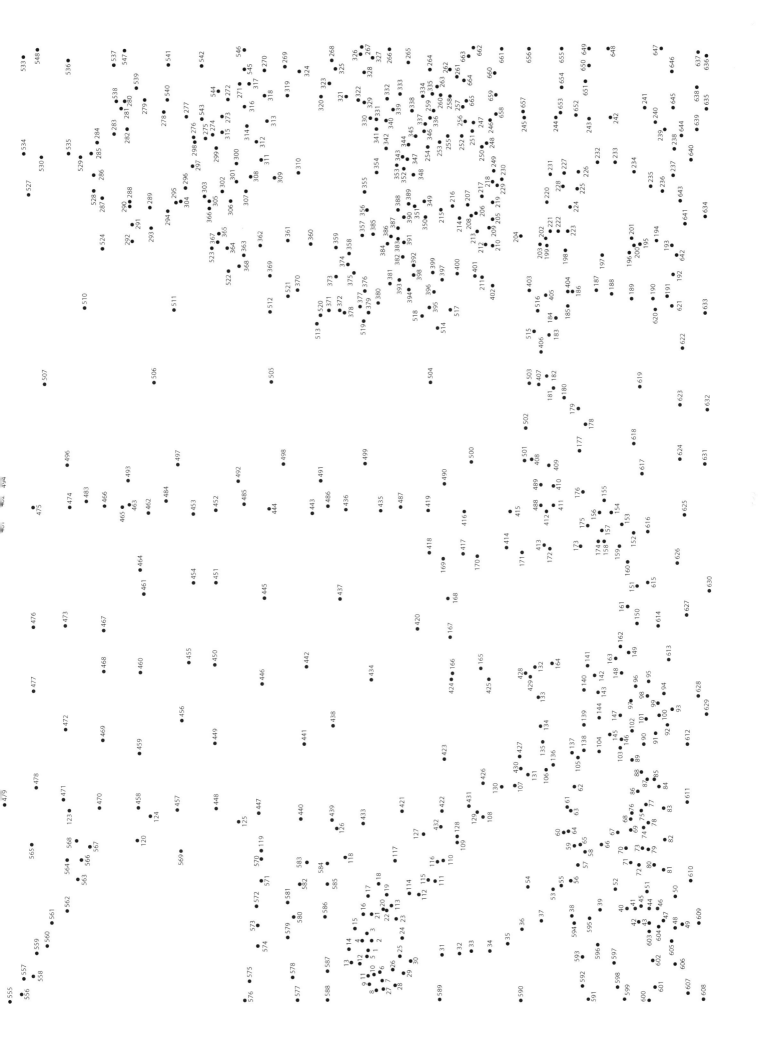

Farm Gardening (511 dots) - Black

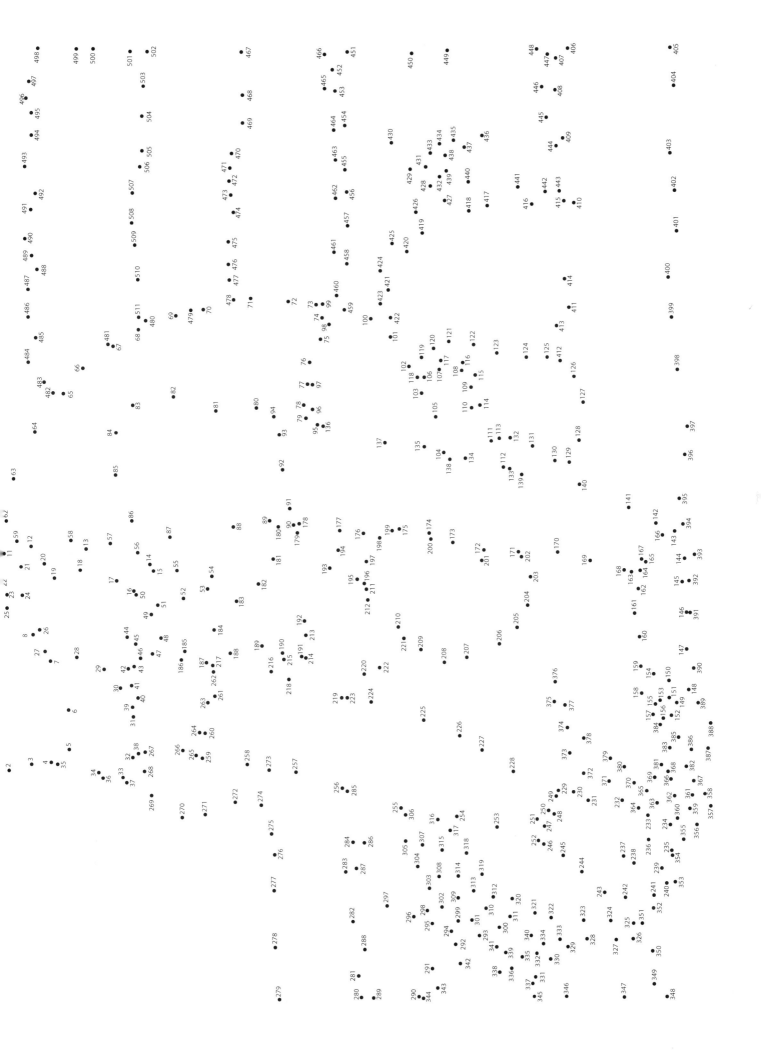

Farmer Couple (643 dots) - Black

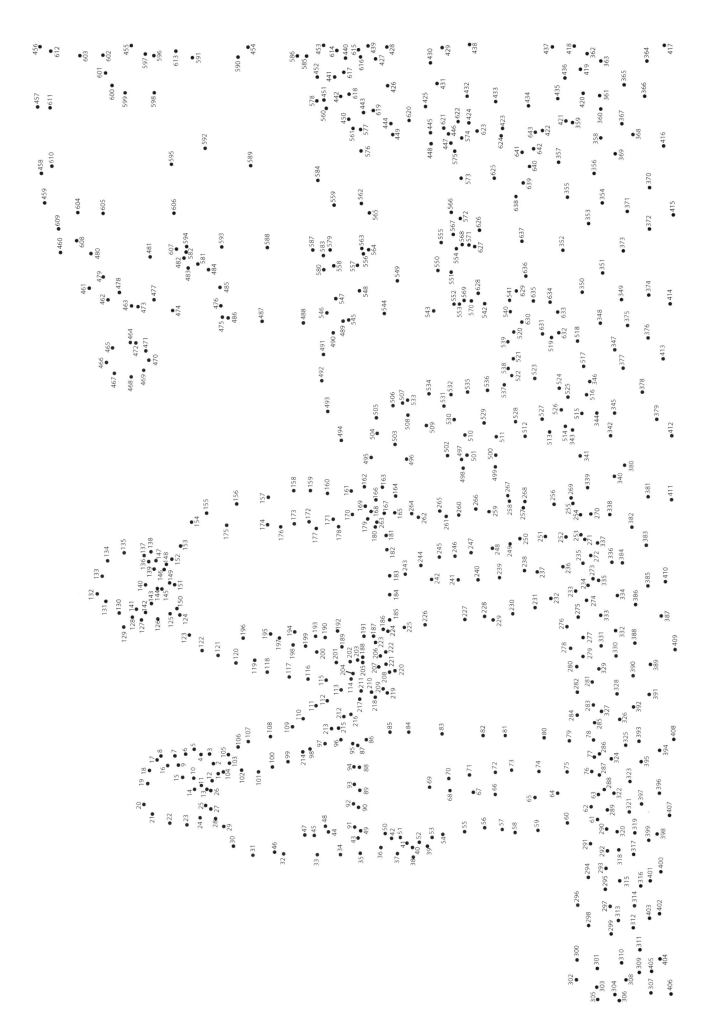

Farmer Farming (559 dots) - Black

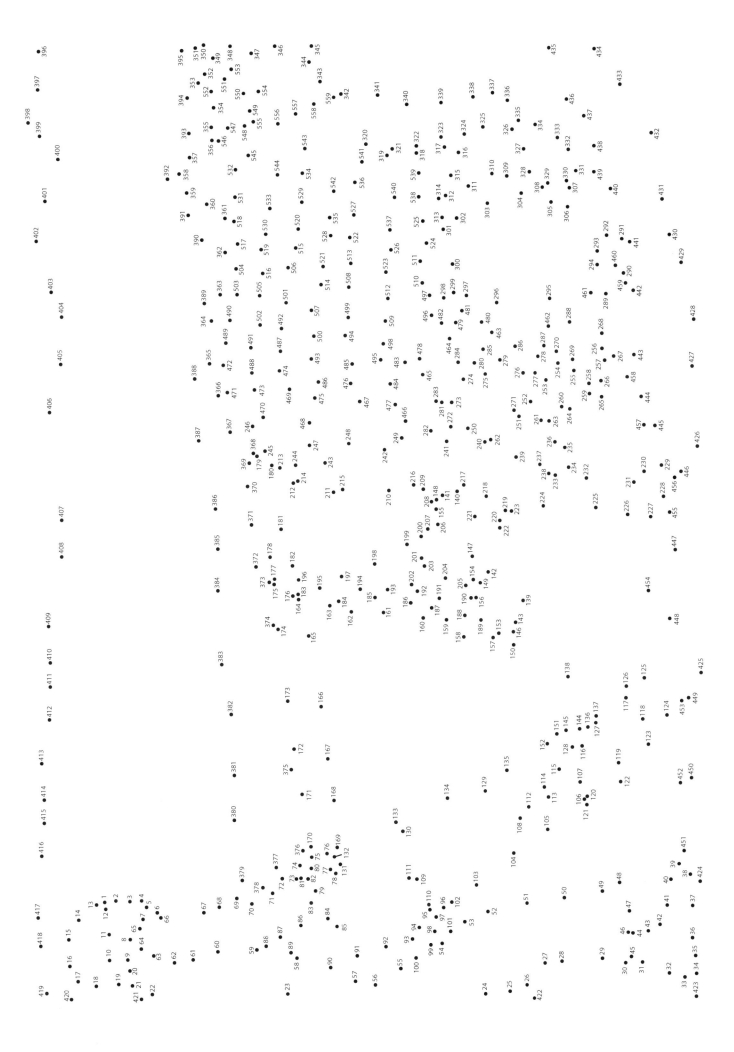

Farmer Picking Cherries (635 dots) - Black

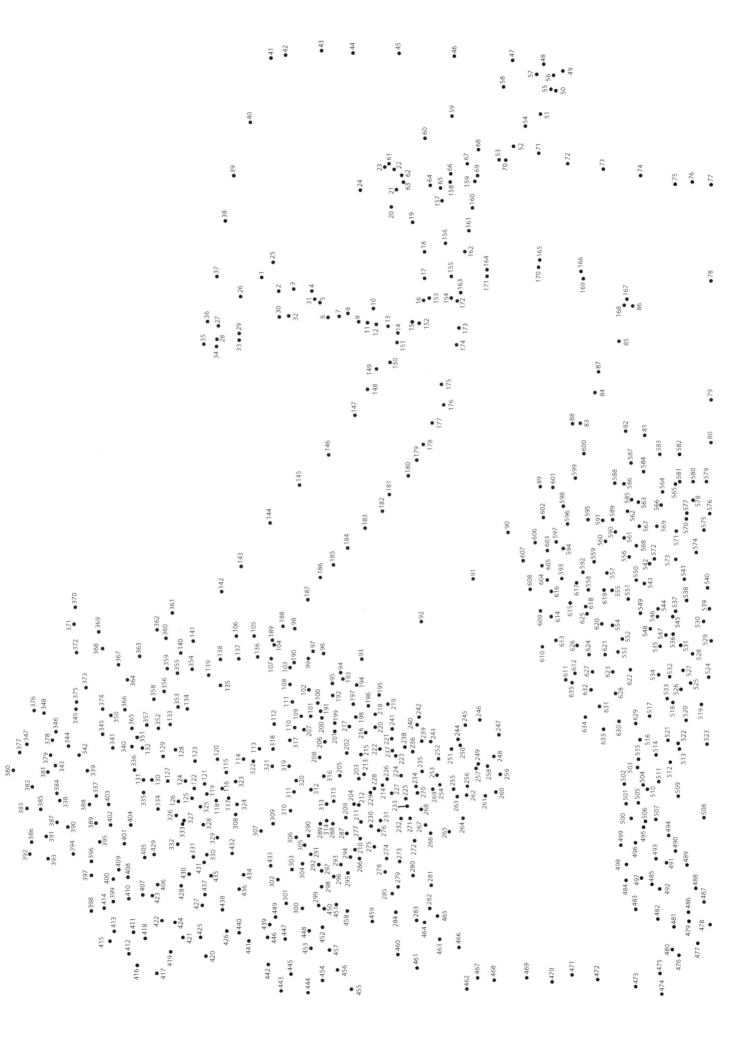

Farmer with Buffalo (536 dots) - Black

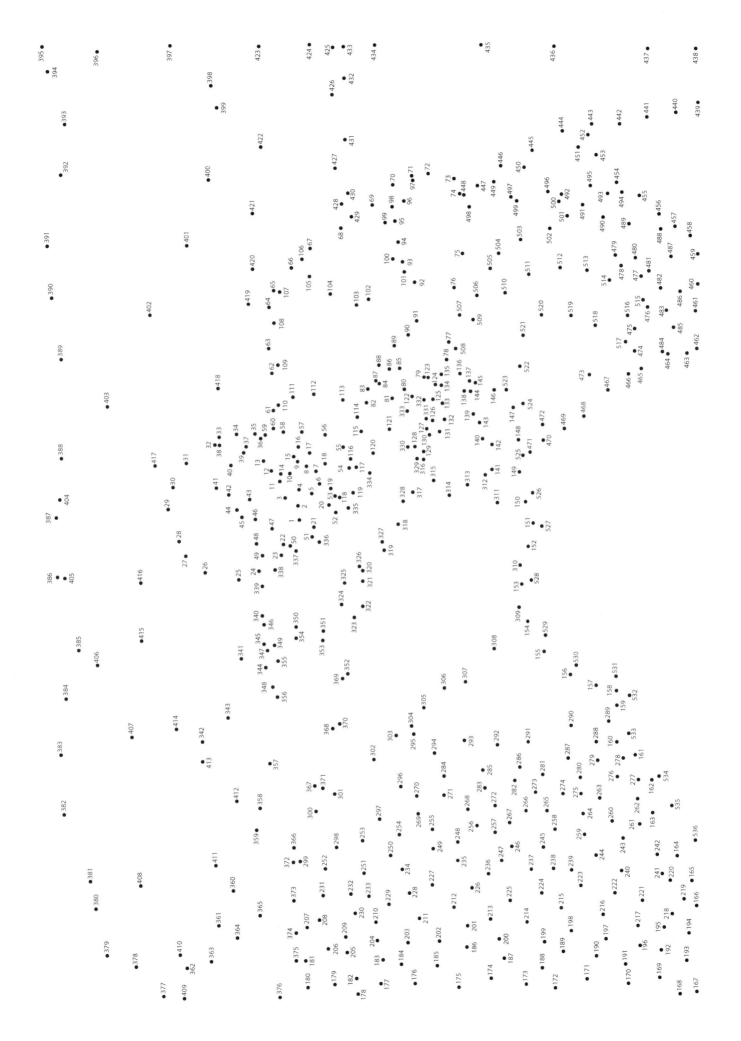

Farmer with Family (619 dots) - Black

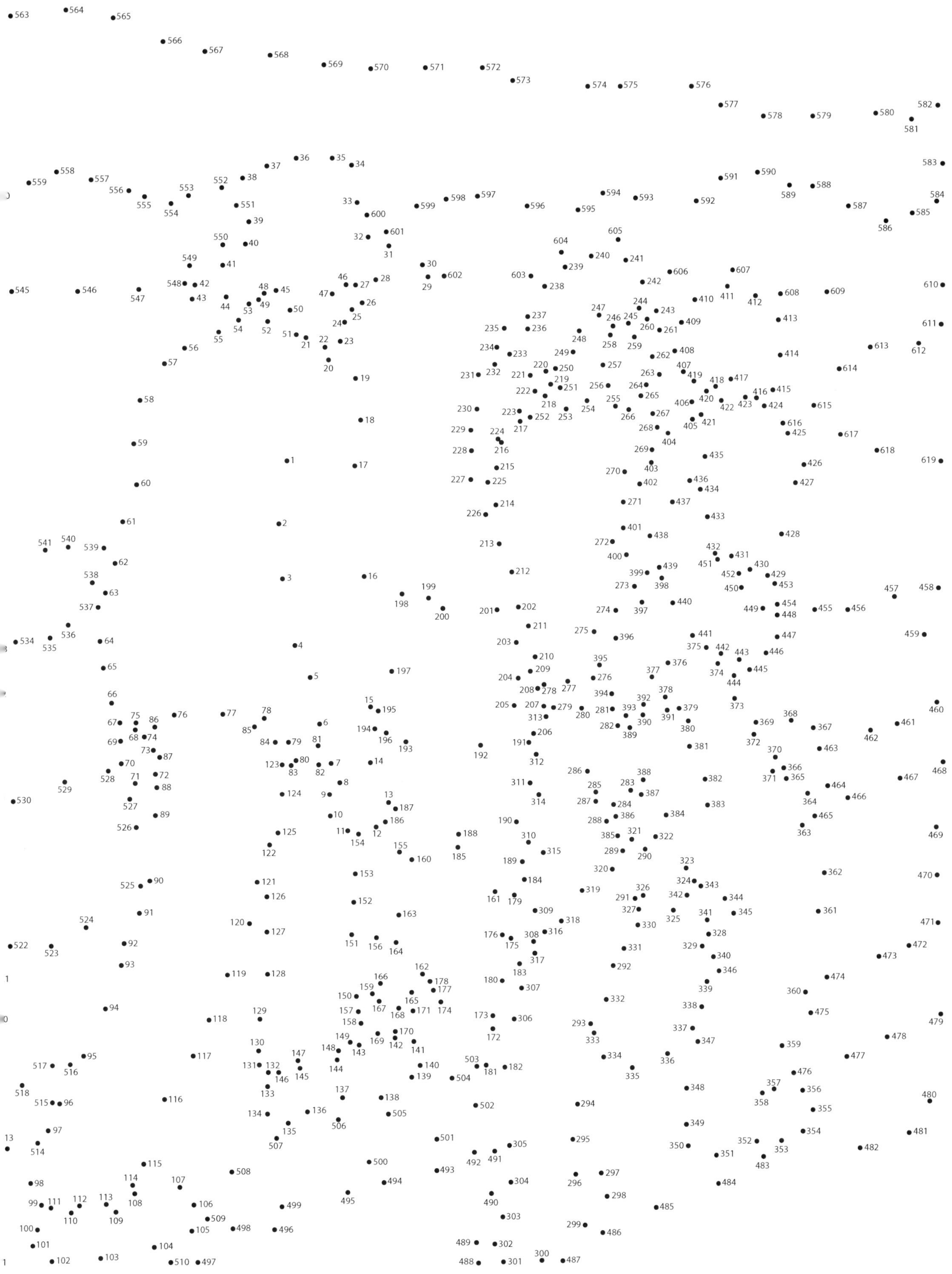

Farmer with his Son (579 dots) - Black

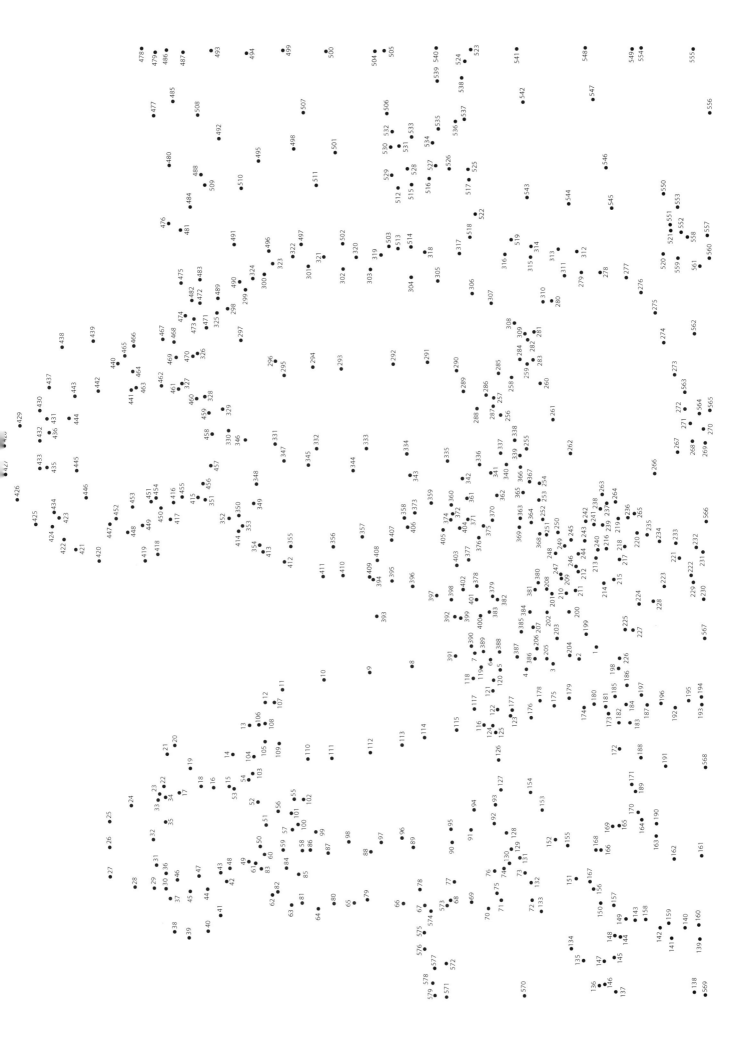

Feeding Cow (501 dots) - Black

Gambrel Roof Barn (505 dots) - Black

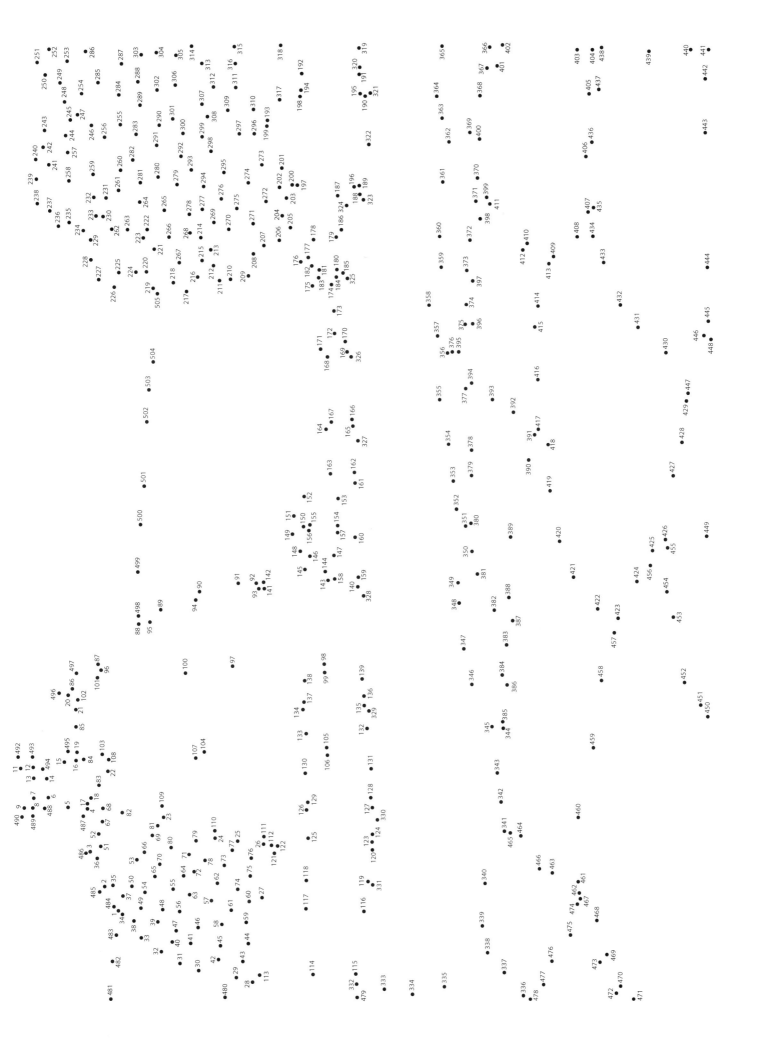

Girl Carrying Vegetables (503 dots) - Black

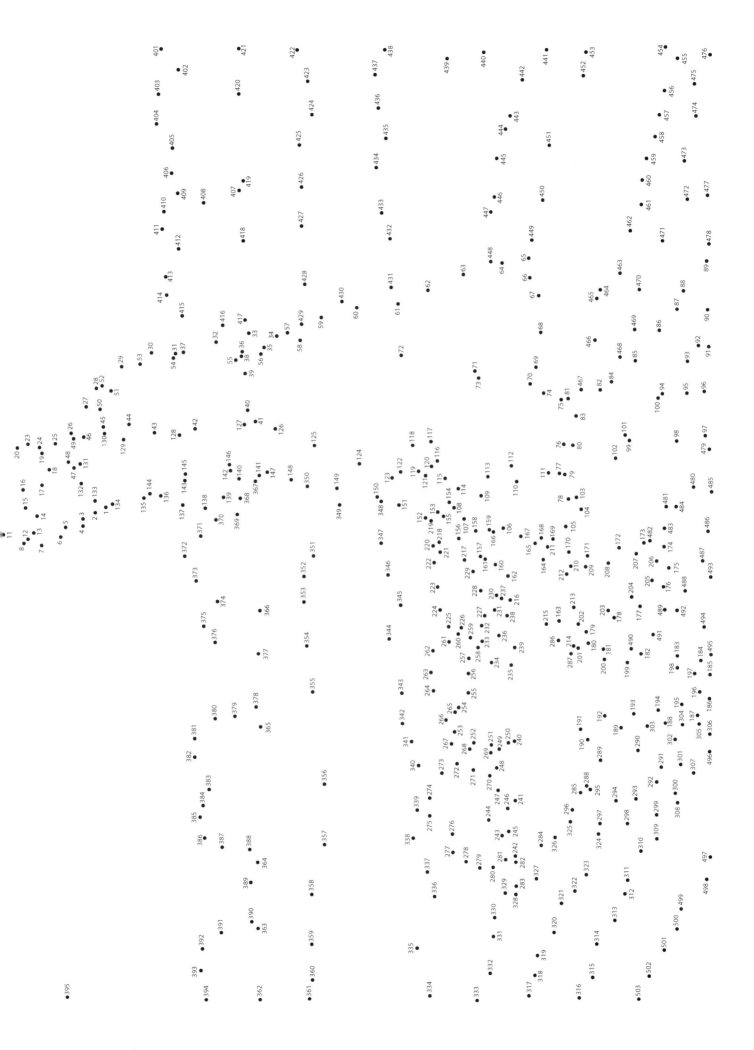

Girl with Chicken (530 dots) - Black

This is a connect-the-dots puzzle consisting of numbered points. The numbered dots are distributed across the page as follows (reading approximately left-to-right, top-to-bottom):

441, 442, 443, 444

305, 445

306

307, 321, 322

304, 308

303, 302, 309, 310, 320

301, 300

311, 316, 33, 34, 318, 163

32, 35, 319

314, 315, 31, 162, 36, 160

30, 161, 159

29, 11, 10, 9, 37

12, 1, 8, 158, 38

28, 2, 48, 7, 39, 156

27, 13, 3, 47, 157, 40, 46

26, 53, 4, 49, 62, 63, 155, 154

313, 25, 52, 5, 50, 45, 42, 41, 69, 153

312, 97, 96, 24, 14, 54, 51, 60, 43, 68, 67, 70, 72, 71, 152

98, 95, 15, 23, 17, 16, 55, 64, 44, 66, 73, 74, 128, 151

118, 94, 20, 18, 59, 65, 75, 76, 127, 150, 164

99, 93, 22, 21, 19, 56, 57, 58, 82, 77, 129, 149

100, 101, 117, 119, 89, 88, 90, 87, 83, 81, 79, 78, 126, 130, 148

102, 92, 84, 80, 125, 131, 143, 147, 168

103, 120, 116, 91, 85, 122, 123, 124, 142, 144, 146, 169

104, 121, 86, 114, 132, 133, 136, 139, 141, 145, 170, 167

105, 115, 113, 134, 135, 137, 138, 140, 179, 180, 181, 166, 165, 327

106, 107, 108, 112, 111, 194, 193, 192, 195, 196, 191, 182, 190, 171, 174, 175, 330, 324

109, 110, 204, 189, 183, 172, 176, 331, 326, 325

297, 298, 296, 203, 205, 295, 202, 201, 200, 199, 197, 198, 185, 178, 173, 177, 332

206, 292, 207, 287, 208, 209, 210, 211, 184, 213, 333, 212, 475

294, 529, 293, 530, 288, 286, 248, 249, 247, 214, 474, 473

528, 527, 526, 525, 524, 285, 250, 215, 476, 472, 471, 470, 469

523, 522, 521, 520, 519, 289, 284, 246, 477, 480, 481, 482, 483

518, 291, 290, 283, 251, 254, 253, 252, 245, 216, 334, 335, 329, 336, 328, 478, 479

517, 415, 282, 255, 244, 217, 337, 488, 487, 486, 485, 484

516, 414, 416, 281, 256, 243, 218, 338, 219, 490, 489, 354

515, 413, 280, 257, 242, 339, 491, 353, 355

512, 417, 412, 258, 221, 220, 224, 352, 356, 361, 362

511, 278, 261, 260, 259, 222, 223, 241, 340, 492, 357, 360, 363

411, 262, 263, 225, 493, 341, 351, 358, 359, 365, 364, 366

277, 240, 226, 342, 350, 367

10, 418, 410, 264, 239, 227, 494, 343, 349, 348, 368

276, 265, 238, 228, 344, 347, 369

409, 266, 237, 229, 495, 392, 345, 346, 370, 381, 382, 371

419, 275, 267, 236, 230, 391, 390, 389, 383, 372, 373, 370

408, 274, 268, 235, 234, 233, 232, 231, 496, 388, 386, 384, 378, 380, 379, 376, 374

09, 273, 269, 270, 271, 272, 503, 502, 501, 500, 499, 498, 497, 394, 395, 387, 385, 377, 375

420, 407, 506, 505, 504, 402, 401, 400, 399, 398, 397, 396

508, 406, 421, 507, 404, 403, 405

22

Girl With Chicken (551 dots) - Black

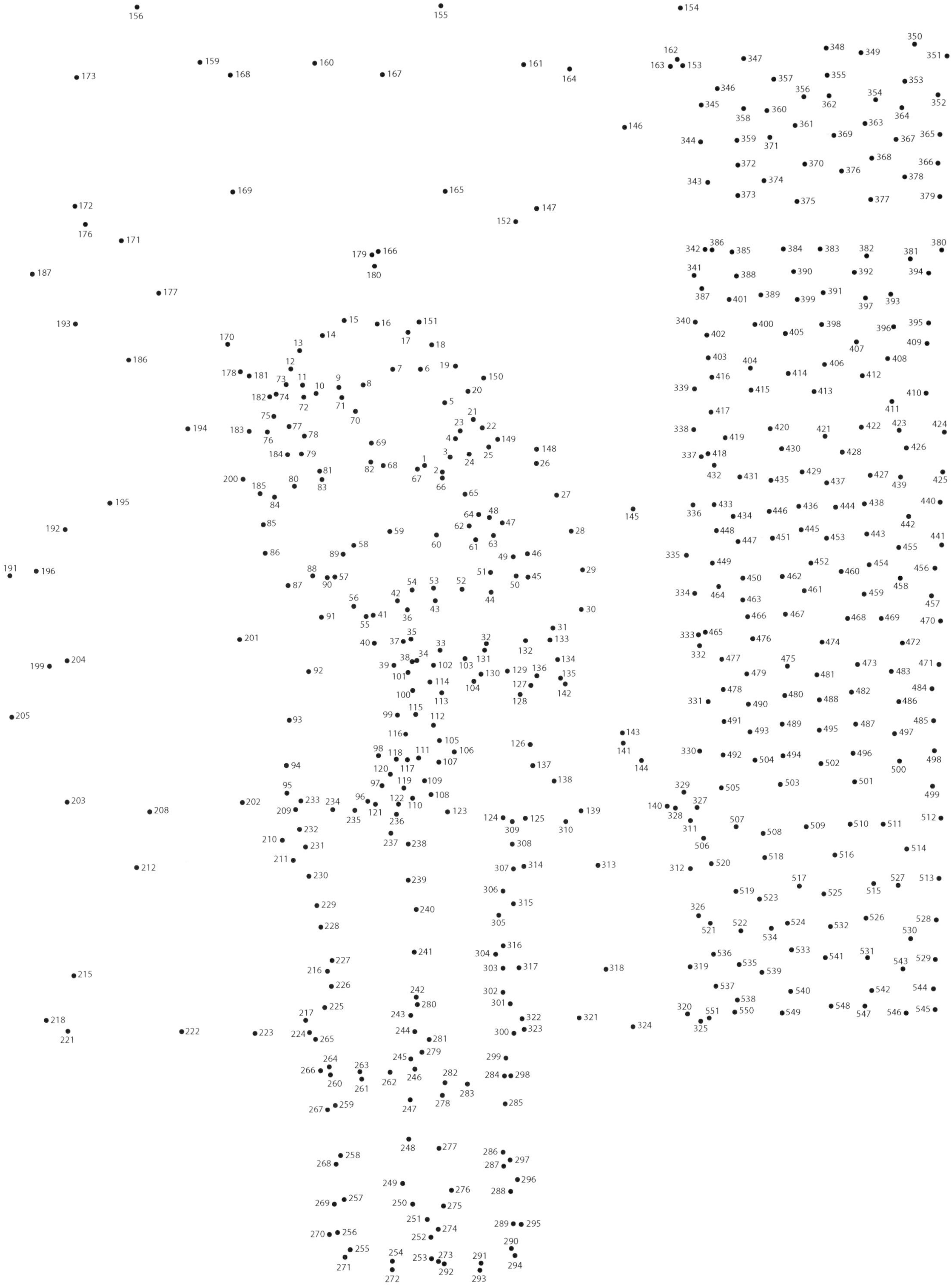

Girl With Horse (505 dots) - Black

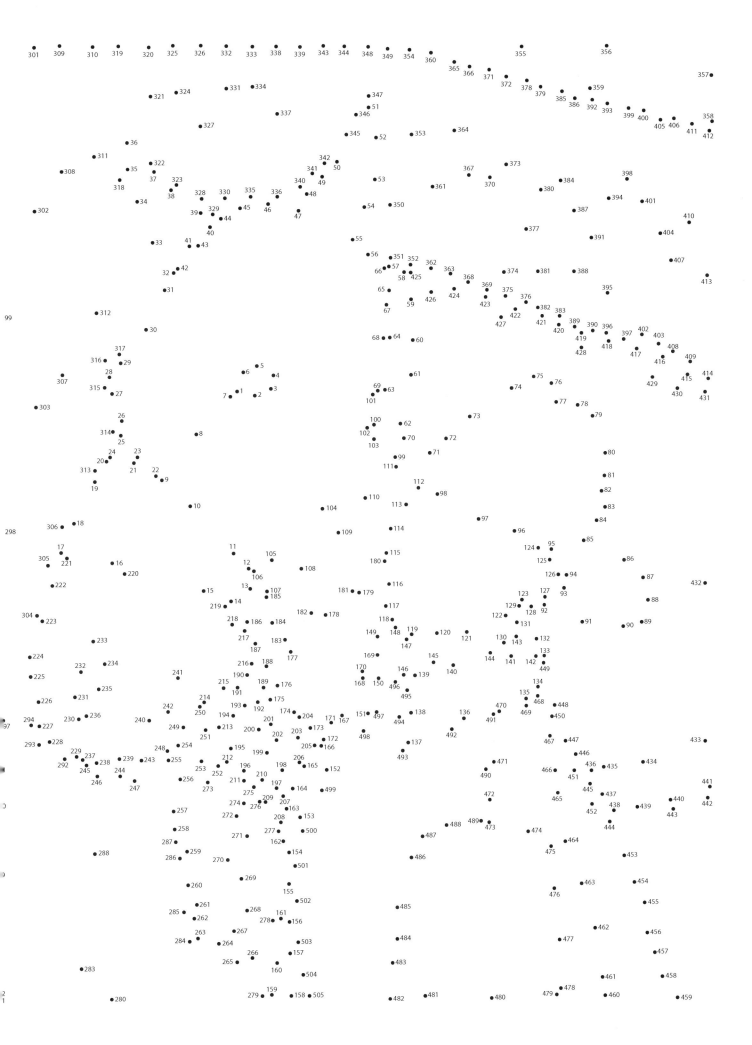

Girl with Sheep (525 dots) - Black

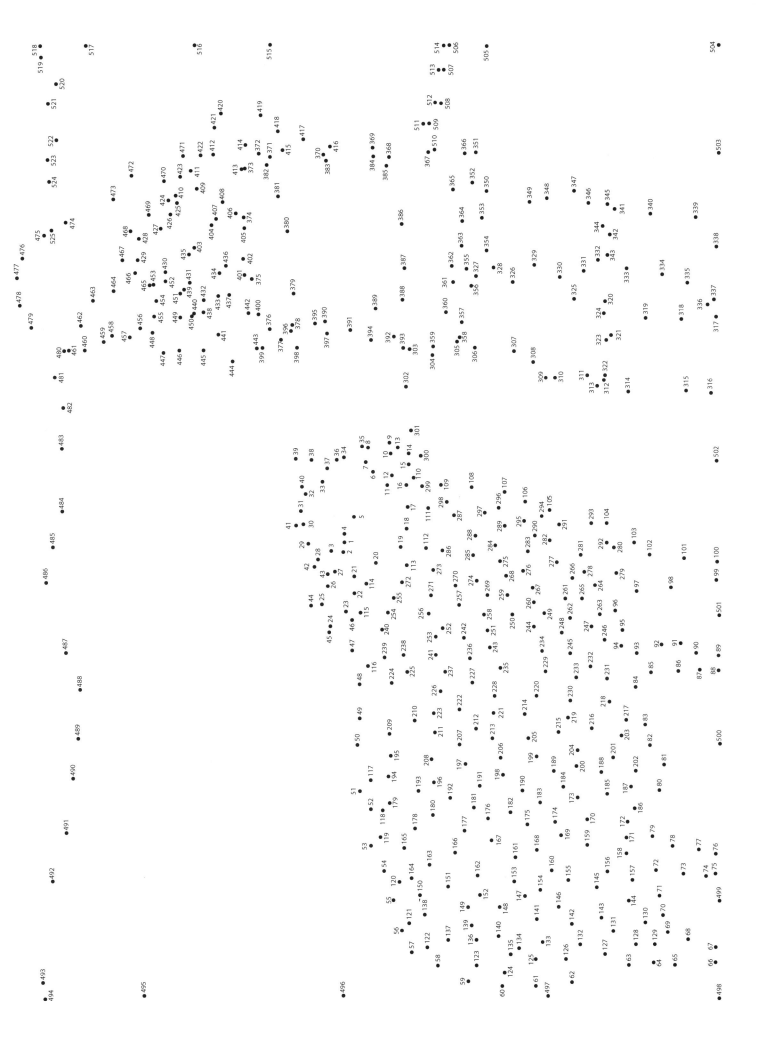

Grandpa and Grandson (689 dots) - Black

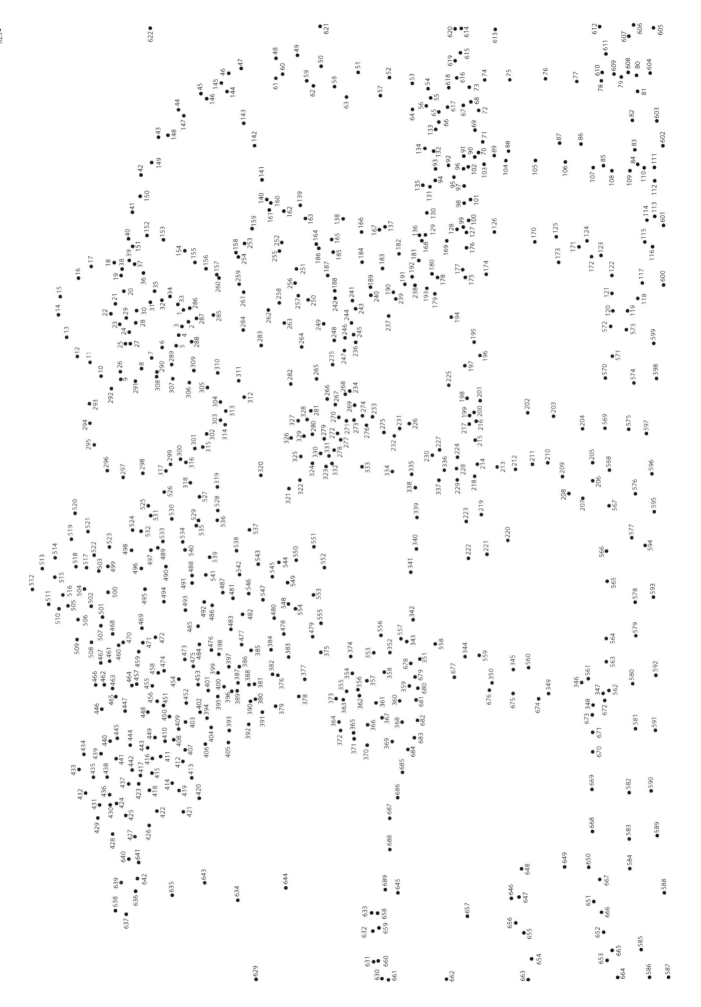

Happy Lady Farmer (555 dots) - Black

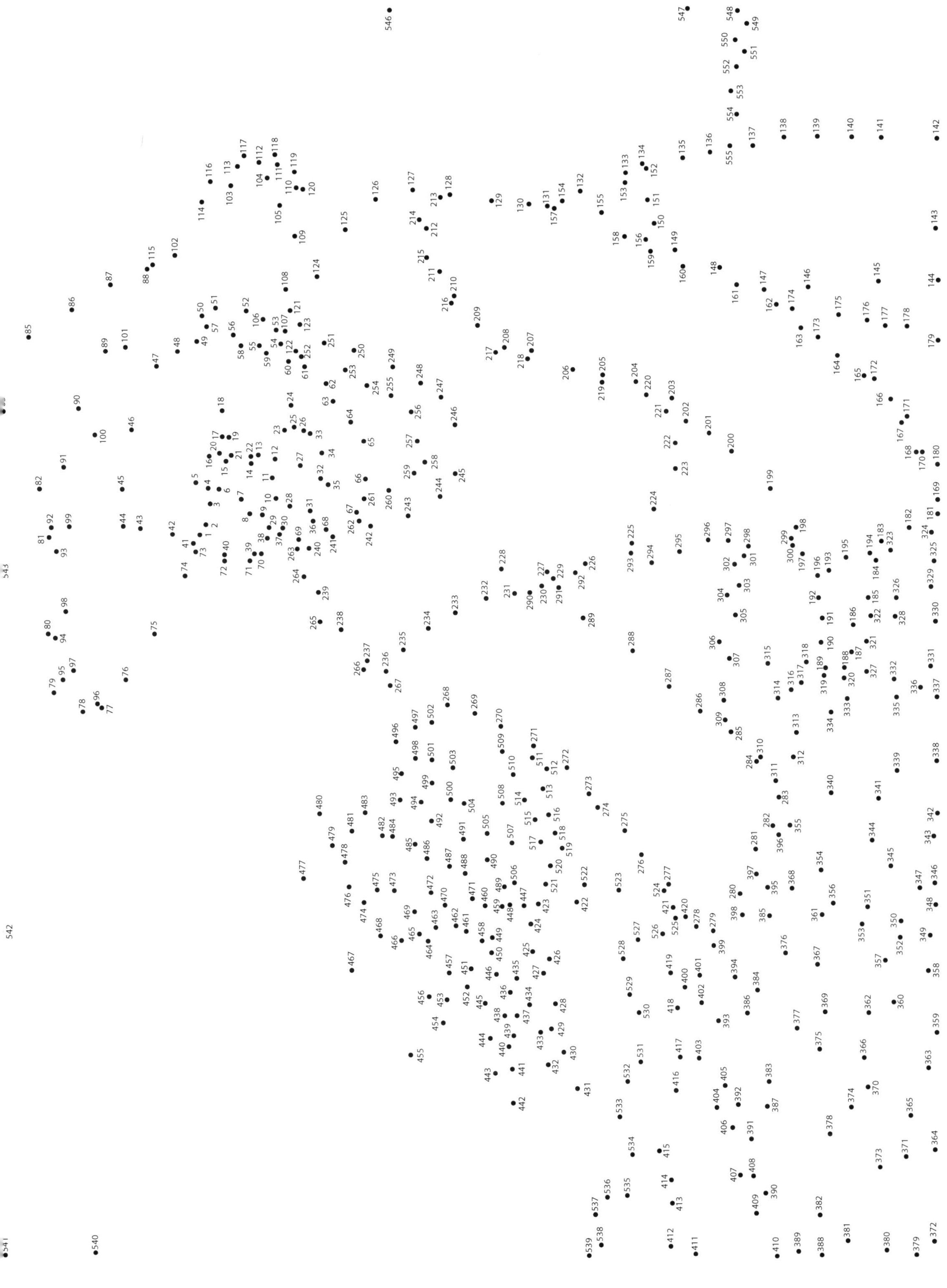

Man Collecting Potatoes (550 dots) - Black

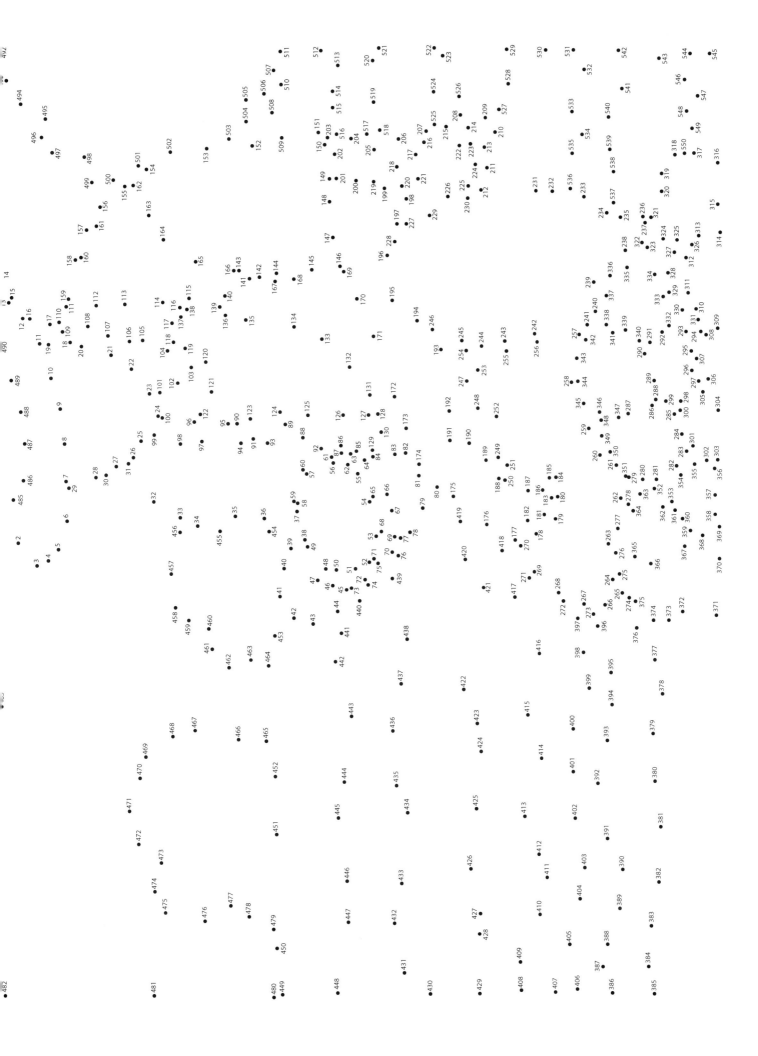

Man Watering (526 dots) - Black

Milking Cow in Farm (602 dots) - Black

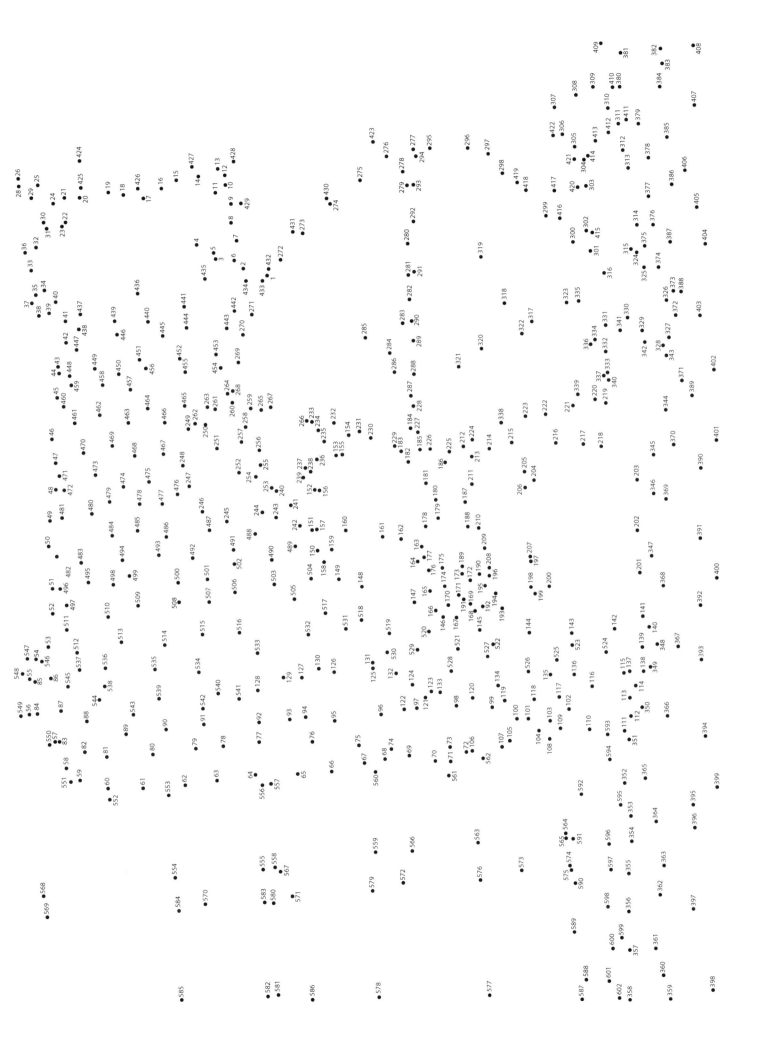

Pig and Hen (602 dots) - Black

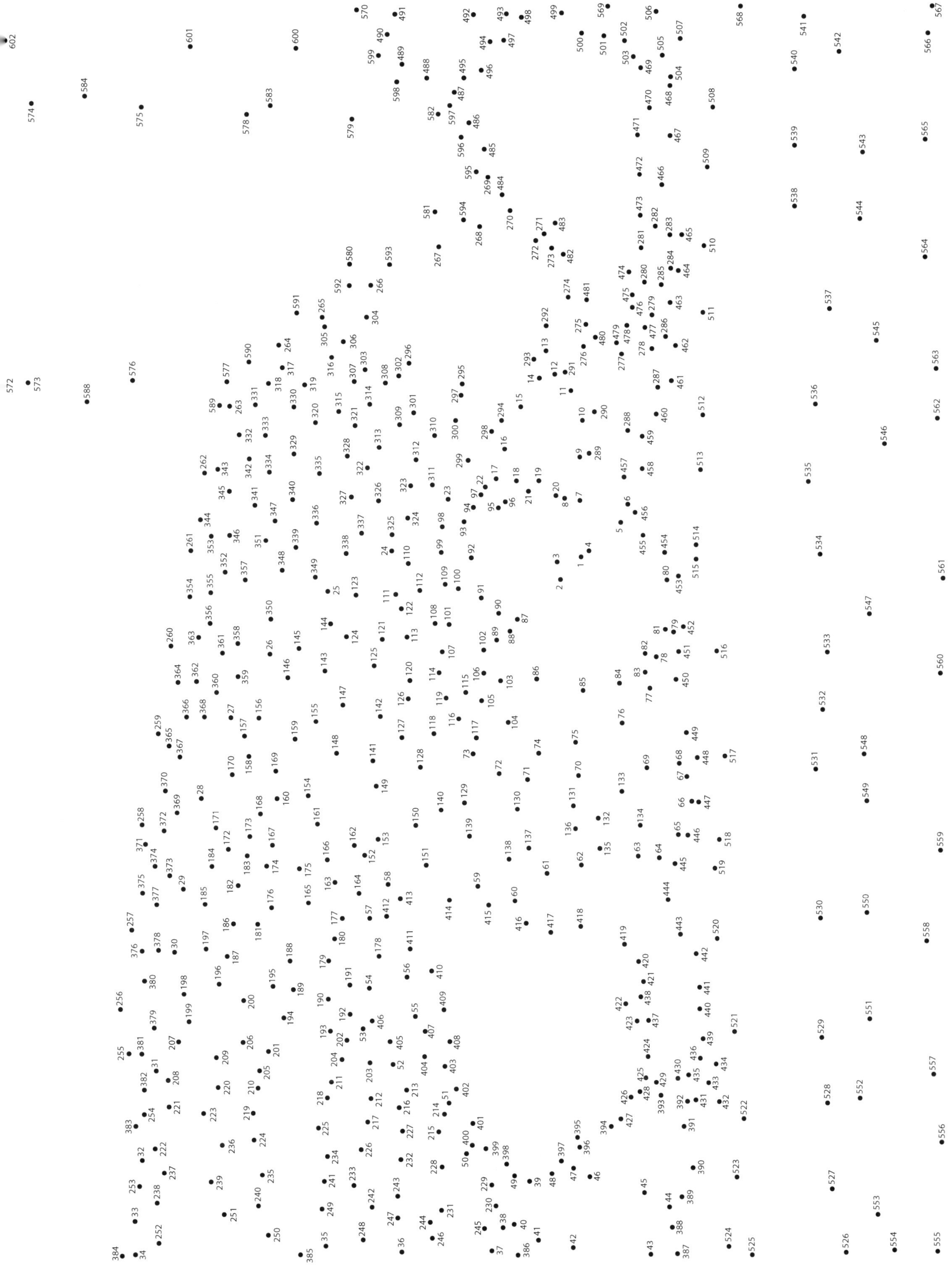

Tractor Farming (662 dots) - Black

56

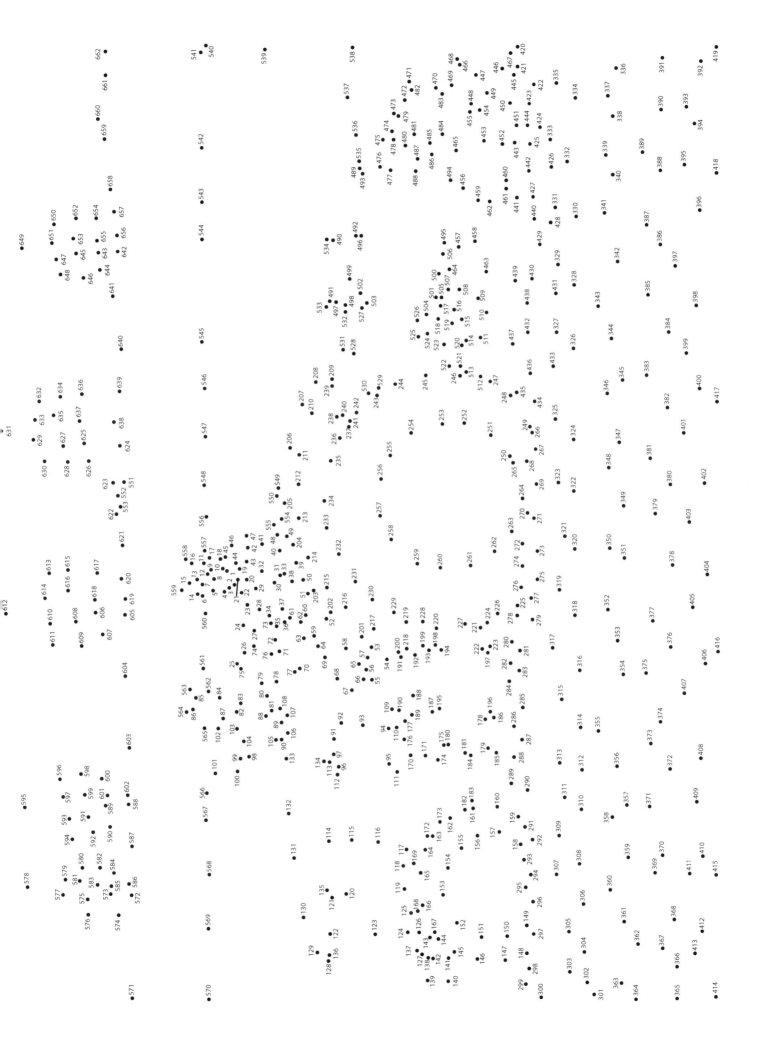

Vegetable Basket (581 dots) - Black

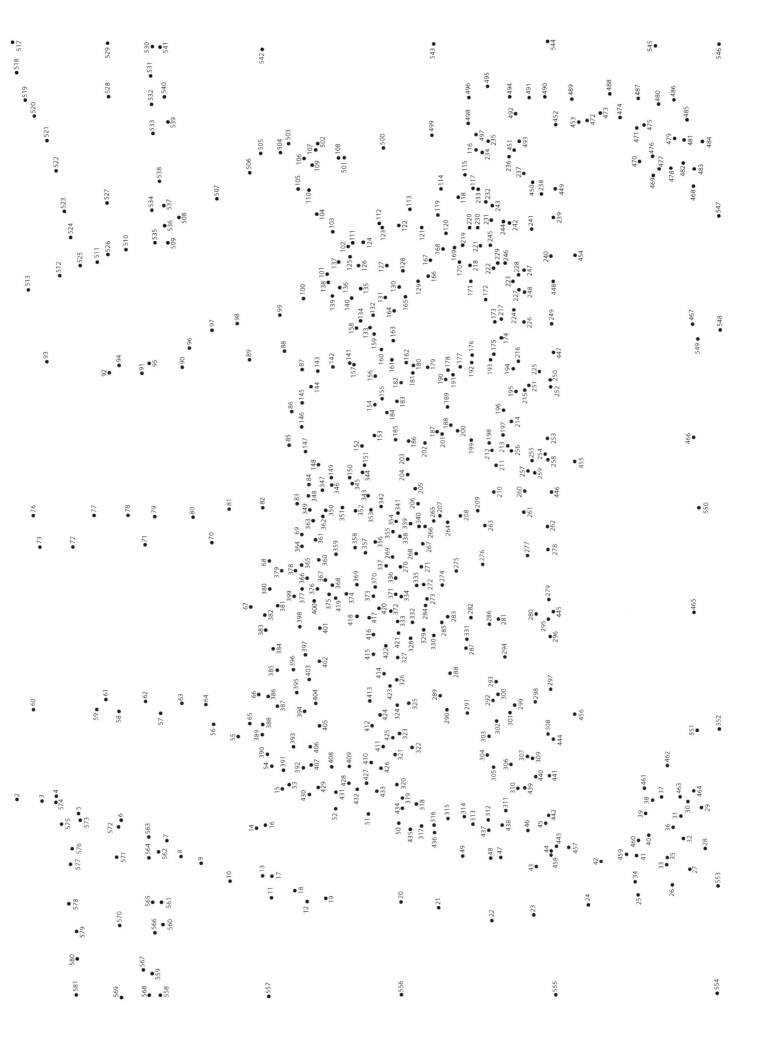

Women Farming (509 dots) - Black

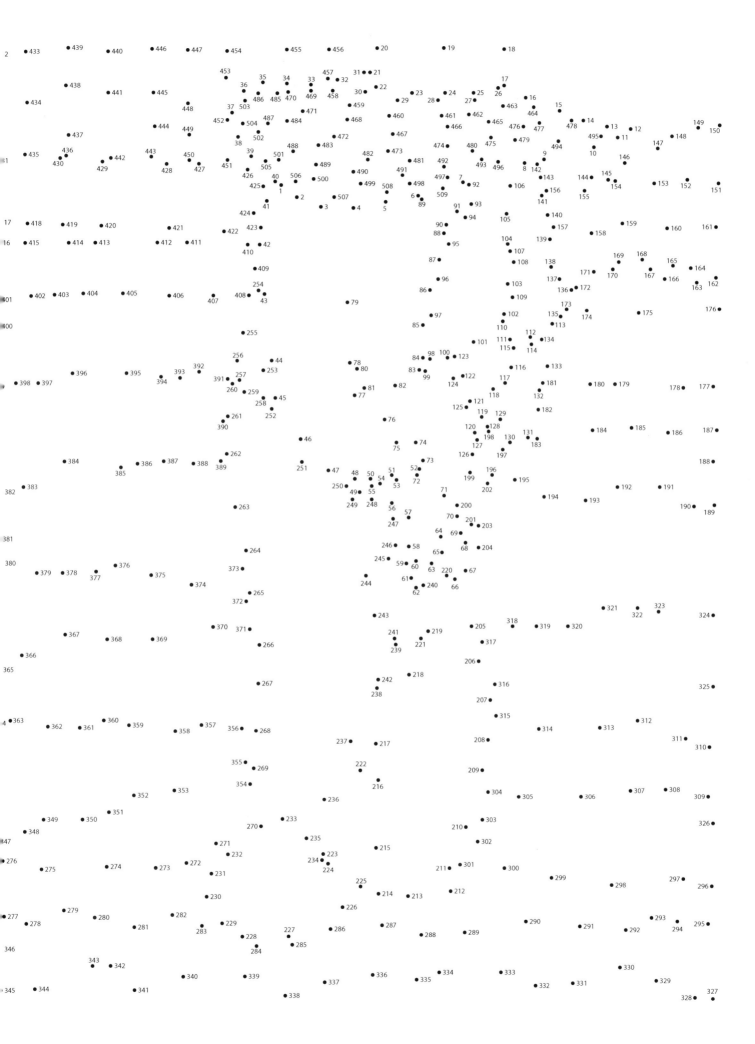

Women Working in Farm (659 dots) - Black

COMPELTED
DOT PAGES PREVIEWS

Completed Dot to Dot Pages Previews

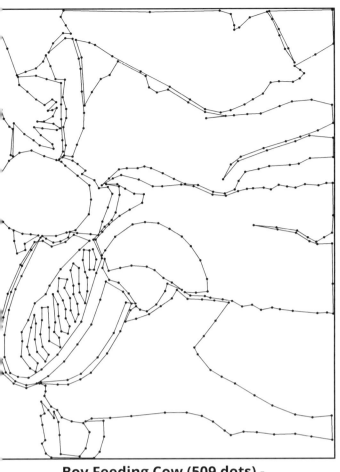

Boy Feeding Cow (509 dots) -

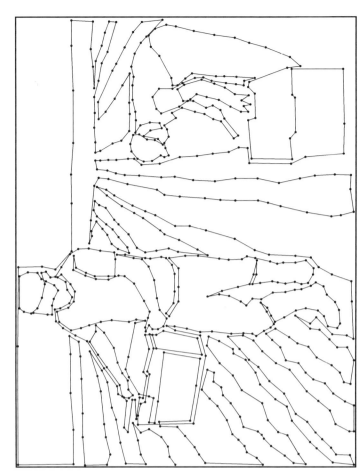

Couple Farming Seeds (650 dots) -

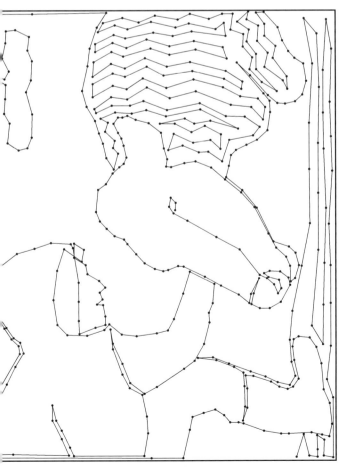

Cow (456 dots) -

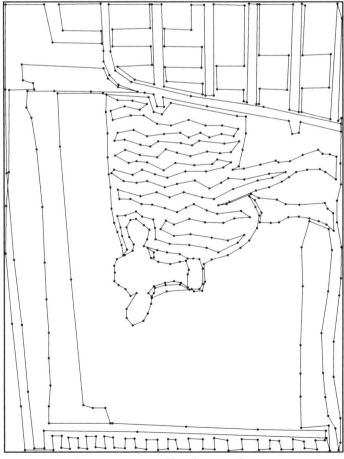

Cow In Farm Shed (475 dots) -

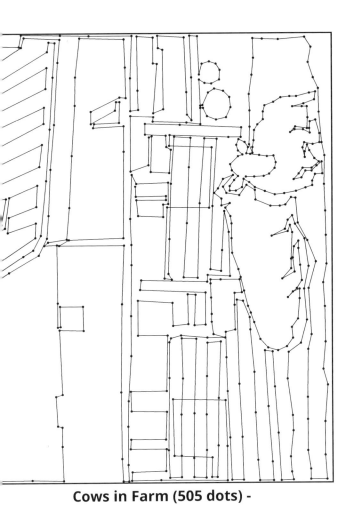

Cows in Farm (505 dots) -

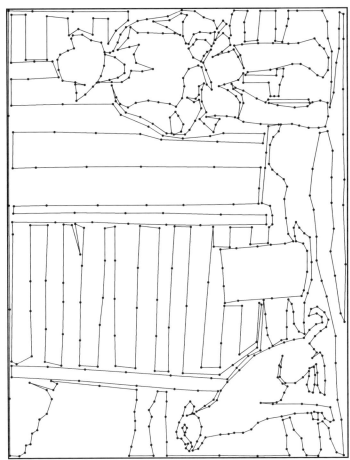

Dog in Farm (665 dots) -

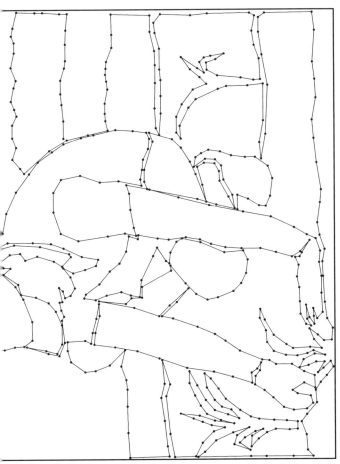

Farm Gardening (511 dots) -

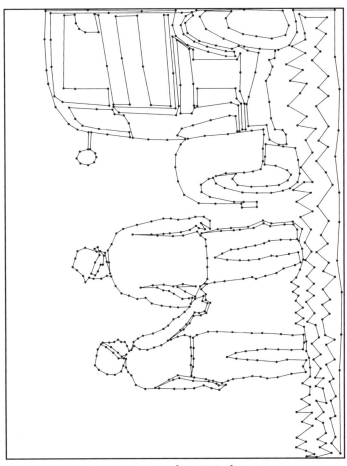

Farmer Couple (643 dots) -

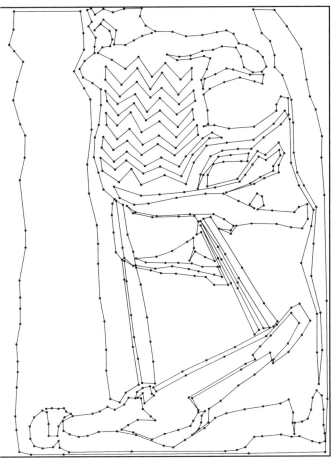

Farmer Farming (559 dots) -

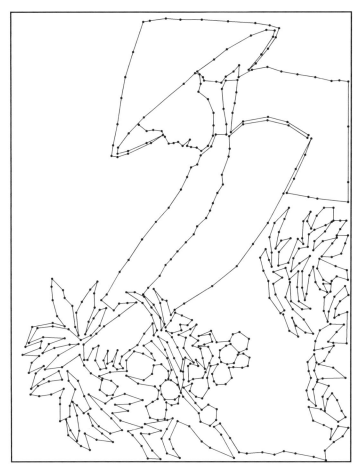

Farmer Picking Cherries (635 dots) -

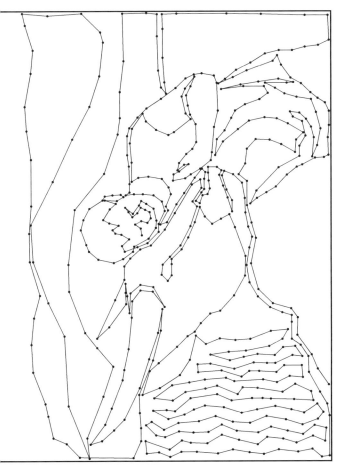

Farmer with Buffalo (536 dots) -

Farmer with Family (619 dots) -

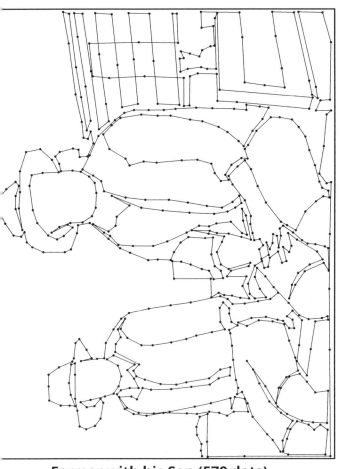

Farmer with his Son (579 dots) -

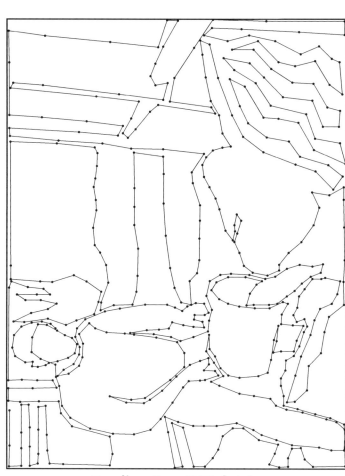

Feeding Cow (501 dots) -

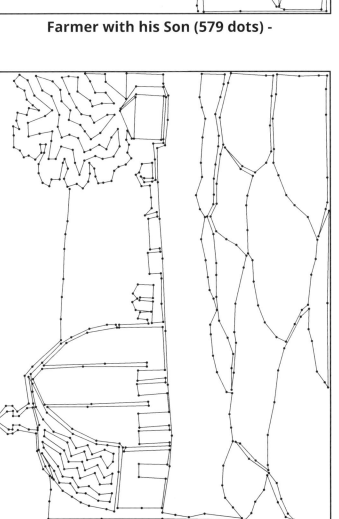

Gambrel Roof Barn (505 dots) -

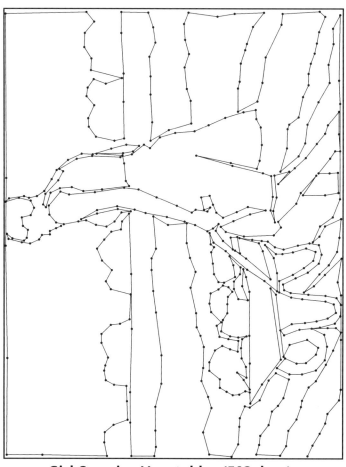

Girl Carrying Vegetables (503 dots) -

Girl with Chicken (530 dots) -

Girl With Chicken (551 dots) -

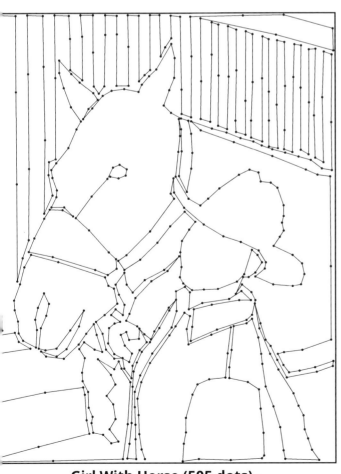

Girl With Horse (505 dots) -

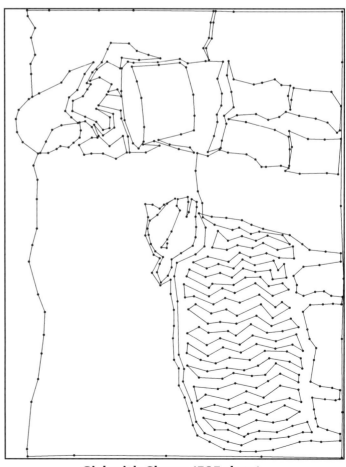

Girl with Sheep (525 dots) -

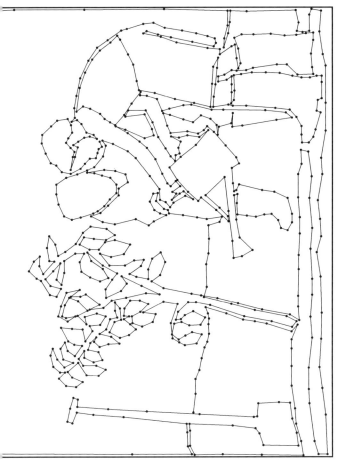

Grandpa and Grandson (689 dots) -

Happy Lady Farmer (555 dots) -

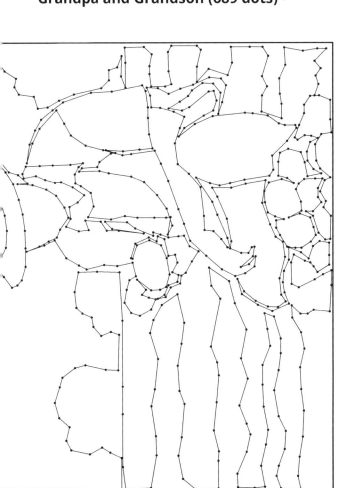

Man Collecting Potatoes (550 dots) -

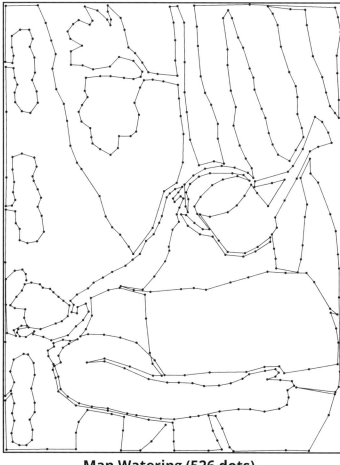

Man Watering (526 dots) -

Milking Cow in Farm (602 dots) -

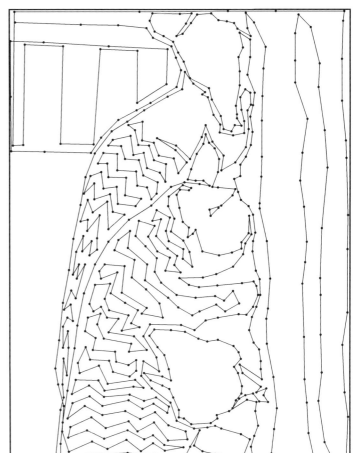

Pig and Hen (602 dots) -

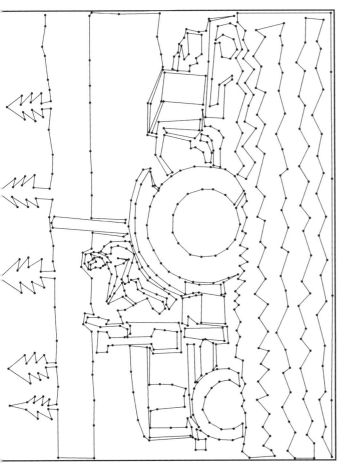

Tractor Farming (662 dots) -

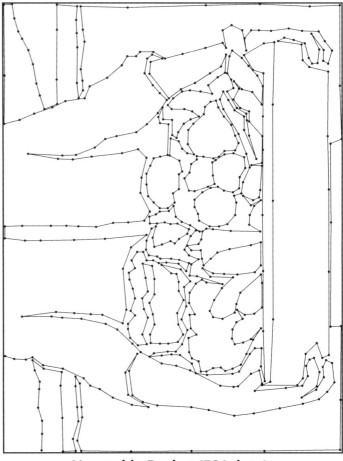

Vegetable Basket (581 dots) -

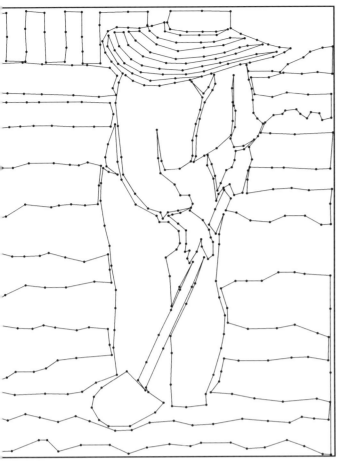

Women Farming (509 dots) -

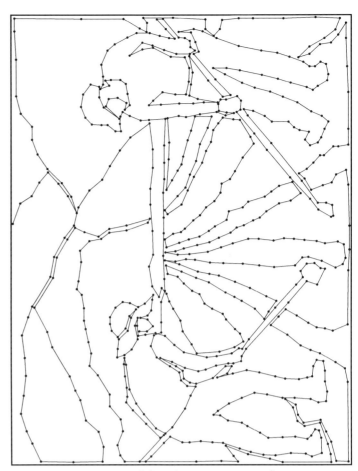

Women Working in Farm (659 dots) -

Made in United States
Orlando, FL
27 November 2024